CHRONICLE BOOKS
SAN FRANCISCO

bugS IN 3-D

by Mark Blum

a^cknowle^dgm^ent^s

In bringing this work to print I have had generous help from many people and I owe them my thanks. I am particularly grateful to A. A. Pennings for contributions too numerous to recite, as well as the donation of his own fine images to this publication. Hugo de Wijs also has my appreciation for the use of his wasp's nest photograph. I remain obliged to my family and friends for their enthusiasm, tolerance, and assistance. For his unsparing entomological consultations, I am indebted to Dr. Harvey Scudder. Mary Henness has earned my respect for mastering her aversion to insects long enough to type my graphic descriptions of their some-times grotesque behaviors. Ben Skeen deserves credit for supplying several of the tropical arthropods that grace these pages. Finally, I wish to recognize my publisher and editor for having the vision to launch this unique series and the faith in me to commission *Bugs in 3-D* even before *Beneath the Sea in 3-D* had sold a single copy.

Printed in Hong Kong

ISBN 0-8118-1945-0

Library of Congress Cataloging-in-Publication Data available.

Book and cover design: Patricia Evangelista.
Grass photograph on the cover and pages 1, 3, and 5 by Ryan Blum.
Plate nos. 21, 22, 25, and 43 photographed by A.A. Pennings.
Plate no. 35 photographed by Hugo de Wijs.

Distributed in Canada by
Raincoast Books
8680 Cambie Street
Vancouver, B.C. V6P 6M9

10 9 8 7 6 5 4

Chronicle Books
85 Second Street
San Francisco, California 94105

www.chroniclebooks.com

preface

You are holding a truly unique book—a portfolio of three-dimensional photographs combined with a stereoscope. Through its lenses, you will pass beyond the boundaries of the printed page to enter the alien world of the insect. Here you will experience the astonishing mosaic of insect life in depth and detail far beyond the limits of normal human vision. This extraordinary effect has been achieved with special 3-D cameras that lend you the visual perspective of an insect, as if your eyes were separated by only a few millimeters. From this rare vantage, elfin bugs loom monstrously into view.

No matter where you live, many of the creatures in this book will be at the same time both familiar and strange. You may recognize the general appearance of numerous common insects, but be quite surprised by the unimaginable details which only macro stereo optics can reveal. Other subjects, like the obscure toad bugs, may appear completely foreign, because their shy habits and minute size normally render them all but invisible to our wide-set human eyes. All but a few of the creatures in this book were photographed in their natural habitats. Seen close-up in 3-D, these small worlds also yield hidden visual surprises.

Many of the creatures featured on these pages are insects belonging to the class *Insecta*, but other terrestrial arthropods such as spiders, scorpions, and ticks are also included. Despite this variety, the text and images in this book offer merely a glimpse of the incredible diversity of insects and their relatives, the most successful and predominate organisms on the planet. Roughly 1,500,000 species of animal life have been scientifically described. Just about one million are insects. While this may sound like a large number, it is estimated from tropical rain forest counts that there may be as many as 30 million species of insects. About six to seven thousand new species are described each year. Unfortunately, mass habitat destruction may be causing the extinction of insect species even faster than they are being classified.

Not only are there a staggering number of species—our planet is teeming with endless swarms of insects: about 200 million for every human being, or 26 billion for each square mile of the earth's surface. As might be expected of such successful creatures, insects have been established for a long time. Their wingless ancestors date back about 400 million years. If the entire history of life on this planet were represented by a single calendar year, insects arrived in mid-October, while humans appeared on New Year's Eve. Over the eons, insects have become essential to every food chain and consequently to all existing life on earth. Without insects, life as we know it would cease.

And now some words directed to bugs of another sort, my fellow shutterbugs, who are characterized by an insatiable appetite for technical facts. Most of the images in this book were photographed at magnifications ranging from one-half to three times life size. They were made with true stereo cameras, meaning both images were captured at the same time. Depending upon the subject distance, the stereo lens spacing (stereo base) varied between two to twenty-two millimeters. For each image, the base was selected to produce a natural (orthostereo) effect without exaggeration.

As stereographers know too well, the economic dictates of today's photographic marketplace do not favor the production of stereo cameras, let alone the specialized macro stereo equipment designed for the production of this book. Consequently, all of these photographs, like those in *Beneath the Sea in 3-D*, were made with hand-built, custom stereo cameras and lenses. These contraptions generally lack many of the features today's photographers have come to expect. The absence of reflex viewing, automatic exposure, automatic focus and zoom lenses, to name but a few modern conveniences, all conspire to make macro photography of wildlife in 3-D particularly challenging and rewarding. Hopefully, new technologies will increase consumer demand for 3-D imagery to a point where manufacturers will one day again produce stereo cameras for the mass market.

I encourage those readers interested in learning more about stereo photography to join one or more stereo associations. Members of the National Stereoscopic Association (P. O. Box 14801, Columbus, Ohio) receive the excellent bimonthly NSA publication, *Stereo World*. For the more technically oriented, membership in the International Stereoscopic Union (c/o Judy Fentress, P. O. Box 19-119, Hamilton, New Zealand) includes a subscription to the quarterly journal *Stereoscopy*. A wealth of information on stereo photography, equipment, and associations can be found on the Web at http://www.3d-web.com. E-mail may be directed to the author at markb@red-shift.com. Those persons interested in purchasing a hands-free viewing stand to hold your copy of *Bugs in 3-D* and the author's other 3-D titles may obtain details by sending a legal size, self-addressed, stamped envelope to the author at 840 Walnut Street, Pacific Grove, California, USA, 93950.

the plates

plate 1

yellow-faced bumblebee

BOMBUS VOSNESENSKII

These widely recognized bees are abundant everywhere, visiting flowers of all kinds. Due to their large size, bumblebees are able to drink nectar from, and thus pollinate, certain flowers that honeybees cannot. This female bumblebee is busy drawing nectar from deep within a large thistle flower. She will return to her colony with a large load of pollen clinging to specialized pollen baskets (corbiculae) on each of her rear legs. Bumblebees self-regulate their body temperature, allowing them to exploit flowers in the cold of early spring and high elevations, where they are particularly common.

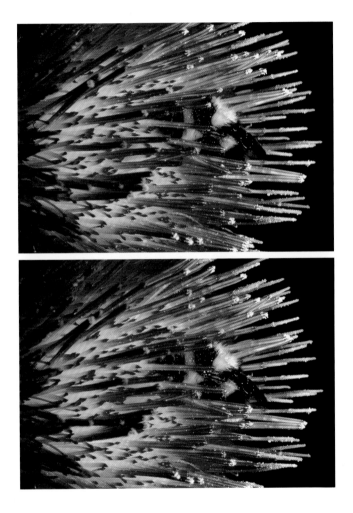

plate 2

Clemence's blue butterfly

ICARICIA LUPINI SSP. MONTICOLA

Butterflies and moths belong to the insect order Lepidoptera. Derived from Greek, the word *Lepidoptera* means "scale wing." Lepidoptera is the second largest order of insects, with 165,000 species distributed worldwide. The familiar life cycle of butterflies from egg, larva, and pupa (or chrysalis) to adult is well known to most people. Butterflies range in size all the way from ⅛th inch to just under 12 inches. The blues, as a group, are relatively small butterflies. Many of these beautiful species of butterflies may be close to extinction. The Xerces Blue, which became extinct around 1943, is the namesake of the butter-fly habitat conservation group known as the Xerces Society.

plate 3

fruit fly

FAMILY TEPHRITIDAE

These distinctive flies are recognizable by the marbled patterning on their wings. Males display these "picture-winged" patterns to females during courtship, and entomologists use the patterns to identify and distinguish among the 4,500 species of fruit fly distributed throughout the world. Many species of fruit fly have become cosmopolitan as a result of the commercial transportation of fruit bearing their hidden larvae inside. Most adult fruit fly species feed on flowers, or are leaf miners. Among the pest species of fruit fly is the notorious Mediterranean Fruit Fly, *Ceratitis capitata*. Other species are beneficial, and are being studied as potential agents for biological weed control.

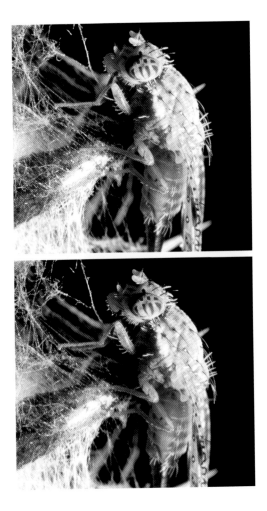

plate 4

Zebra tarantula

APHONOPELMA SEMANNI

As with all the tarantulas, the Zebra tarantula is a hunting spider. It forages at night for live prey. Sense organs on its numerous body hairs are highly sensitive to vibration. The tarantula's small eyes are poorly developed and only register changes in light levels. Its powerful front legs are used to restrain prey, which is then subdued with a downward thrust of the large, hairy fangs (chelicerae) visible in this image. While most of the 30,000 known species of spiders have venom glands, it is surprising to learn that only about 30 species worldwide are capable of poisoning humans. The bite of a tarantula can be quite painful, but the venom is usually mild, and rarely fatal.

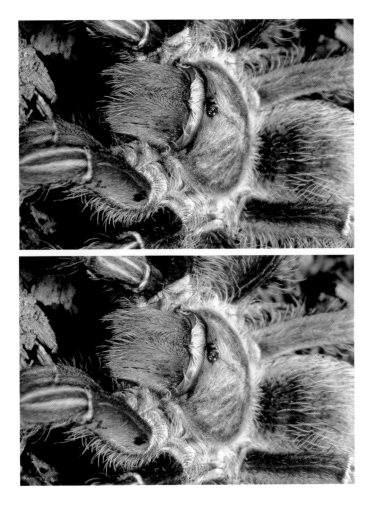

plate 5

tarantula hawk

PEPSIS THISBE

The Tarantula Hawk is the largest member (up to 1⅞ inches long) of the spider wasp family (Pompilidae), in which all species prey on spiders. When the female spider wasp is ready to breed, she locates a spider, wrestles the spider over, and paralyzes but does not kill it with a sting to the underside. The spider wasp then digs a hole (some species dig the hole in advance or use a spider's own lair), places the stunned spider inside, lays a single egg on its abdomen and buries the spider alive. When the young wasp larva hatches, it drinks the paralyzed spider's fluids, pupates, and later digs out of the hole as an adult wasp. The Tarantula Hawk feeds on milkweed nectar and can deliver a very painful sting.

plate 6

mating soldier beetles

FAMILY CANTHARIDAE

Soldier beetles are recognizable by their long, nearly rectangular-shaped bodies ending in a downward-pointed head with sharp, curving jaws. The thin wing covers (elytra) are soft and covered with short, downy hair. The long antennae are threadlike. This mating pair of beetles was photographed during daylight hours, when soldier beetles are commonly seen on plants. Note in the photograph how the male has locked his forelegs below the female's head and appears to hang from her larger body. Adults of most species feed on other insects, but some eat pollen and nectar. The soldier beetle larvae are always predatory.

plate 7

Common Water Strider

GERRIS REMIGIS

These curious, semi-aquatic insects in the family Gerridae are found all over the world. With their long legs and claws, they skate over the water on depressions in the surface film, noticeable in this image. The water strider's middle legs act as oars while the front legs are superbly adapted for catching insects on the water surface. The feet and body are covered with water-repellent hairs that aid flotation. Other hairs are sensitive to vibration, allowing water striders to detect their prey. Water striders will sometimes attack each other, particularly when the victim has just molted. Whether adults will develop wings appears to depend on whether their aquatic home is subject to drying up, requiring migration to a new habitat. Species of the genus *Halobates* are adapted to marine environments and may be found up to 150 miles out on the open ocean.

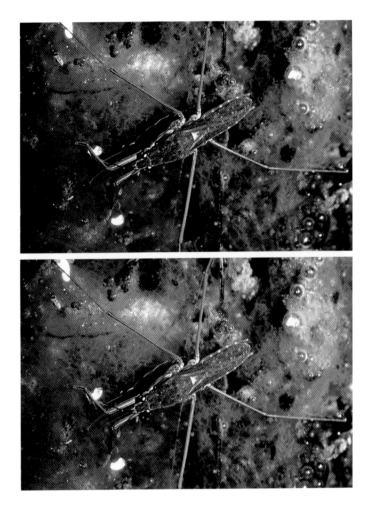

plate 8

Scorpion

CLASS SCORPIONES

This specimen is a true scorpion of the class Scorpiones, recognized by its large pincers and the long tail with a poisonous stinger at the tip. Depending on the species, the scorpion's venom can range in potency from completely ineffective to lethal. Scorpions eat other arthropods and are found worldwide. The female carries her eggs in a sack attached to her abdomen. When they hatch, she carries her offspring around on her back, feeding them "milk" from her ovaries. The young scorpions become independent after their first molt.

plate 9

spiny bellied orb weaver Spider

MICRATHENA SP.

This view from beneath a typical orb-weaving spider reveals much of the generalized structure of spiders. The eight legs common to all spiders emanate from the sternum. Immediately above the sternum is the white labium. Above to the right and left are the maxilla. The short pair of leg-like structures are the pedipalps. The black spot on the abdomen immediately below the legs is the simple booklung. Below the booklung is the epigyne and immediately beneath it is the epigastric furrow opening into the reproductive organs. At the tip of the abdomen are the prominent spinnerets, the external openings of the silk glands.

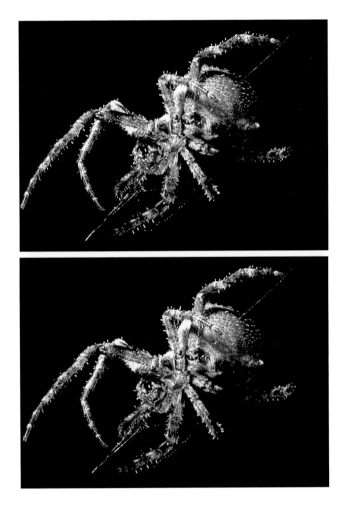

plate 10

common laceWing

CHRYSOPA SP.

As their name implies, lacewings are recognizable by their four wings with many cross-hatched veins. They are in the order Neuroptera, a name derived from the Greek words for "nerve" and "wing." All lacewing larvae and the adults of most species feed on mites and small soft-bodied creatures. Lacewings particularly like to eat aphids, and are therefore friends to gardeners. Because they are mainly active at night, some adult lacewings have a bat-avoidance mechanism—receptors in their wings are sensitive to the ultrasonic sounds made by bats. The Common Lacewing lays eggs that are each supported above a leaf on a slender stalk. This structure protects the very weak and delicate larva as it emerges from the egg. At this point in time, the larva is too delicate because of its initially unhardened cuticle to defend itself from its brethren, who hatched earlier and are now down on the substrate, ready to cannibalize any potential food, including lacewing larvae.

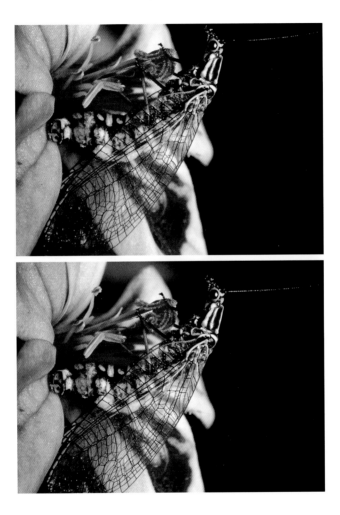

plate 11

dragonfly nymph

FAMILY AESHNIDAE

Dragonflies develop in three stages: egg, nymph, and adult. The developmental process from nymph to adult can take from several months to as long as two years and require as many as 15 successive molts to reach maturity. The nymphs, also known as naiads, are aquatic. Like the adult dragonflies, they are highly predaceous, feeding on crustaceans, amphibians, and fish. When prey is within reach, the nymph grabs it with jaws on a hinged facial mask beneath the head. The strike is lightning fast, lasting just $1/25,000$th of a second.

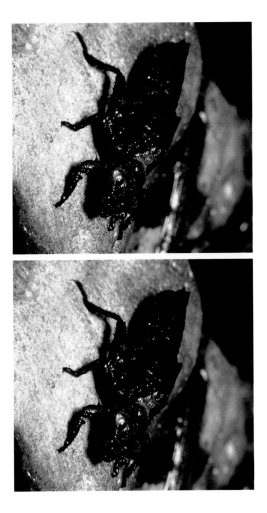

plate 12

dragonfly molt

FAMILY AESHNIDAE

After the dragonfly larva's last molt, the empty outer shell, or exoskeleton, is left clinging to an aquatic reed. The white tracings visible in the photograph are the linings of the air ducts, or tracheae. The exoskeleton is a cuticle largely made of the incredible material known as chitin. All arthropods utilize this multipurpose material, which is also formed into hairs, sense organs, eye lenses, jaws, and flexible hinges between body parts. When pigments are added, chitin is produced in a rainbow of colors. Chitin's very structure may reflect different colors, as in the wings of many butterflies.

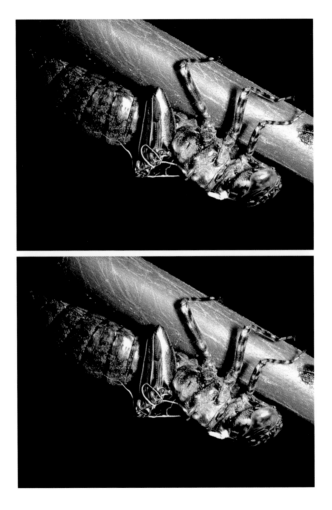

plate 13

newly emerged dragonfly

FAMILY AESHNIDAE

The last molt of the dragonfly naiad results in the newly emerged (teneral) adult pictured here. The new dragonfly will take a few weeks to fully mature. During this time it will leave the water in search of abundant insect prey, venturing as far as 150 miles. When the female is ready to mate, she will return to the aquatic habitat where she was hatched. Although flight in the dragonfly is powered by relatively primitive direct flight muscles, it is nevertheless spectacular to behold. Who has not marveled at the superb high-speed acrobatics of dragonflies giving chase to each other, or catching prey on the wing. When it rests, the dragonfly may angle its wings toward the sun in order to capture solar radiation in the dense pattern of veins that give the wings their structure.

plate 14

mating dragonflies

FAMILY AESHNIDAE

This mature pair of dragonflies demonstrates the characteristic "wheel" mating position. The male grabs the female with his legs and locks the claspers at the end of his abdomen behind her head. The female then swings up her abdomen to be fertilized by secondary sex organs on the front of the male's abdomen, where he has previously transferred his sperm. Before he deposits his sperm, the male scrapes out the sperm of other males from the female's organs. The female is usually ready to lay her eggs (oviposit) right after mating. Depending on the species, she may lay her eggs under the water, insert them in aquatic plant material, or simply scatter them.

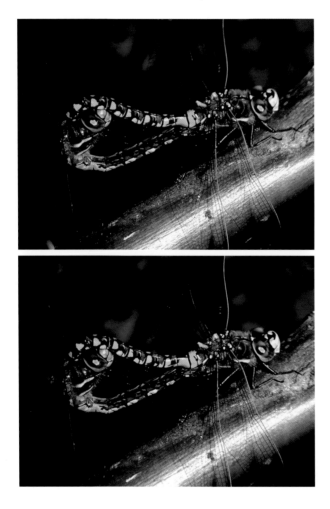

plate 15

painted lady butterfly

VANESSA CARDUI

Like most adult butterflies, the Painted Lady feeds on the nectar of flowers. Most of the adult butterfly's brief life (only one or two weeks for most species) is spent in search of this readily digestible energy source. However, the proteins required for the repair of body tissue, and for females to develop eggs, comes from food reserves stored when the butterfly was still a caterpillar. Also known as the Thistle Butterfly, Vanessa cardui is reportedly the most widely distributed butterfly in the world. The Painted Lady is a sporadic migrant, periodically moving in great numbers. Unlike the well-known migration of the monarch, however, the Painted Lady does not return to the area from which it migrated. In California, where the migrations are northward, the migrating colonies normally die out during the winter.

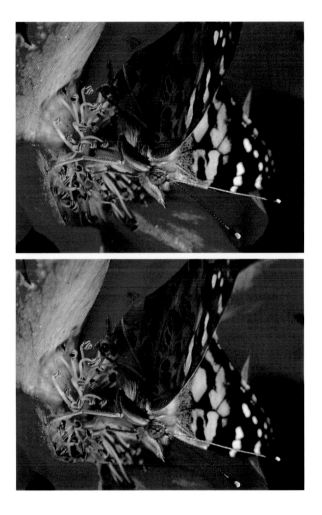

plate 16

tussock moth caterpillar

ORGYIA SP.

This beautiful caterpillar in the family Lymantriidae derives its common name from the tussocks of hair that protrude from its back and sides. The bright coloration advertises to predators that this caterpillar is unpalatable. The body hairs of some species are irritating and will produce an itchy rash. Adult Tussock Moths have a short life span and do not feed. The females of some species are wingless. Being unable to fly, they lay eggs on the same cocoon from which they emerged.

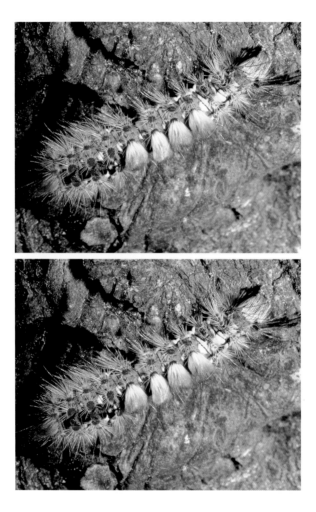

plate 17

Crane fly

TIPULA SP.

Just behind the forewing of the specimen in this photograph you can see one of the club-tipped structures known as halteres. The hind wings of all two-winged, or true flies, are modified into a pair of these balancing structures. The halteres act like gyroscopes, beating in opposite rhythm to the forewings. As the fly changes attitude or course, the stem of the halteres is twisted by the heavier tip. This movement transmits information to the brain, instructing the fly how to adjust its flight path. Mating in crane flies is accomplished tail to tail. The male's abdomen twists 180 degrees to allow his claspers to grip the female.

plate 18

earwig

FORFICULA AURICULARIA

The common name *earwig* has its origins in an old superstition. Many people have long believed that earwigs crawl into people's ears at night in order to bite them. In fact, earwigs are harmless. The pincers at the end of their abdomen are used in defense and to help fold the hind wings beneath the wing covers. Although many earwigs have wings, most are flightless. Earwigs are omnivorous, eating not only vegetables and fruits, but also mites and insects. The female of this species lays up to 30 eggs and stays with them until a few days after they hatch.

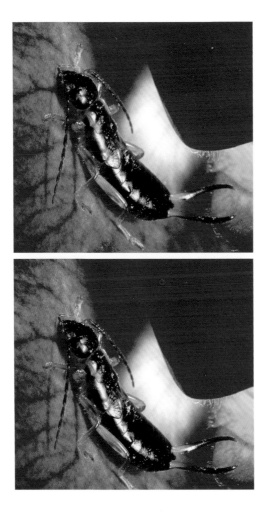

plate 19

mating toad bugs

GELASTOCORIS SP.

These strange-looking little bugs are easy to overlook, as they are quite small (about ⅜ths of an inch) and resemble a small pebble on the shore of a pond or watercourse. Look for the toad bug along the margins of lakes, rivers, and streams. You may see one as it hops away frog-like at your approach. Upon close examination, the toad bug has the warty appearance of a toad. The strong forelegs are useful not only for grasping a mate during breeding, as seen here, but for capturing the small insects upon which the toad bugs feed.

plate 20

dragon-headed katydid

EUMEGALODON SP.

The Dragon-headed Katydid is one of 5,000 known species in the mainly tropical Tettigoniidae family. The armored spines behind the head and on the legs of this large species from Peninsular Malaysia provide it with an excellent defense and can easily draw blood from a person's hand. The long hind legs are modified for jumping and the femur is always longer than the abdomen. Katydids have specially adherent soles, making them excellent climbers. Like their 300 million-year-old ancestors, many adult members of the primitive Tettigoniidae family are carnivorous, feeding on other insects. Because they are dependent upon specialized environments, katydid species are often found in small island-like areas of distribution and are particularly sensitive to habitat loss. Male katydids stridulate, or sing, by rubbing together files and scrapers on their front wings, and each species has its own unique song. Their ears are located on the forelegs.

plate 21

Stink bug

PENTATOMA RUFIPES

If you've ever disturbed a stink bug, then you may have learned how it earned its common name. When threatened, the stink bug may emit a foul-smelling liquid that repels predators and reportedly causes headaches in some people. In the young bugs, or nymphs, these stink glands are on the back of the abdomen. As the bugs mature, other glands on the thorax take over production of the defensive secretion. While the majority of stink bugs drink plant sap, P. rufipes is a carnivore. This particular specimen was photographed feeding on its usual prey, the larvae of another insect. Stink bugs lay their eggs on leaves in a mass which sometimes resembles the cells of a honeycomb. The barrel-shaped eggs are armed with spines in order to deter predators.

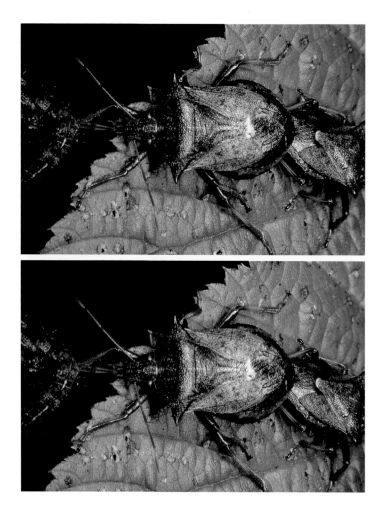

plate 22

red admiral

VANESSA ATALANTA

These butterflies are also known as Brushfoots, because the front legs are physically non-functional. In females, however, the front legs may contain chemical sensors that help to locate host plants for egg laying. Red Admirals produce two or more broods each year. The host plants are often nettles, which have stinging hairs that deter some potential caterpillar predators. The caterpillars fold the nettle leaves together into a nest with a silken thread and may pupate inside. Here the Red Admiral is using its long, tubular proboscis to feed on flower nectar. If enough nectar sources are available, strong adults may overwinter.

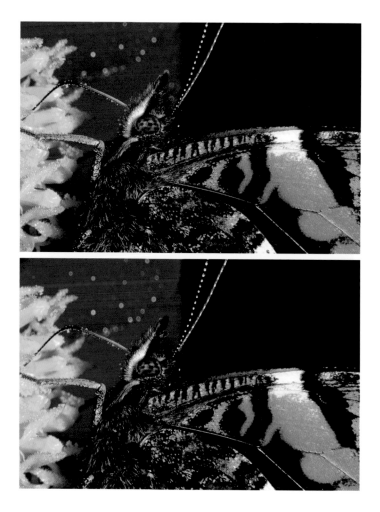

plate 23

stick insect

HETEROPTERYX DILATATA

The stick insect family Phasmatidae includes the longest of all insects, which can grow up to thirteen inches in length. Their legs are designed for climbing and walking, not jumping. Stick insects have the chameleon-like ability to change color in response to shifting light, temperature, and humidity. Like leaf insects, they disguise themselves by hanging motionless from the foliage they can so closely mimic. When disturbed, they may let themselves drop. In addition to its great size (approximately 8 inches), the pictured specimen has strong, sharp spines to deter predation by lizards, birds, and spiders. If attacked, stick insects may shed their legs and regenerate them. Male stick insects are extremely rare, and entirely unknown in many species. Consequently, reproduction from unfertilized eggs, called partheno-genetic reproduction, is frequent. In contrast to the wingless species living in the United States, many tropical stick insects are fully winged.

plate 24

hard-bodied tick

FAMILY IXODIDAE

Ticks are not insects, but arachnids of the order Acarina. These small creatures are recognizable by their oval forms and unsegmented abdomens. This tick is a female, whose hard shield does not cover her entire cephalothorax, allowing it room to expand for egg storage. Adult ticks wait on vegetation for a host to jump onto. This specimen, photographed on the author's forearm, has not yet fed. When engorged with blood, she will swell spectacularly in size. When the tick penetrates the skin, a barbed shield (the hypostome) prevents retreat until the punctured skin of the host has disintegrated. Because many tick species are carriers of disease, it is important to closely inspect yourself for the uninvited presence of these parasites when hiking in fields or other likely tick habitats.

plate 25

drone fly

ERISTALIS TENAX

Like other members of the hover fly family, this species introduced from Europe is able to hover motionless above flowers while feeding on the nectaries. This feat is achieved with an extraordinarily fast wing beat—up to 1,000 beats per second. Two sets of muscles are attached to the drone fly's thorax. The thoracic walls are springlike; when the muscles contract, the thorax vibrates and the wings beat at a far higher frequency than any direct muscle contraction could achieve. The drone fly gains a degree of protection against some predators by mimicking the appearance of a honeybee. Spiders, however, are not fooled by this ruse and will quickly attack a drone fly. The larvae of Eristalis tenax, known as the Rat Tailed Maggot, is semi-aquatic. It develops underwater, but breathes from the surface with a snorkel-like tube over two inches long.

plate 26

rose-hair tarantula

GRAMMONTOLA CALA

Tarantulas are large arachnids in the family Theraphosidae. As a group they are commonly known as "bird-eating spiders," but more often they dine on insects, other spiders, reptiles, and amphibians. The venom of most tarantula species is relatively mild. With such large and powerful bodies, these spiders do not need strong toxins in order to overcome and kill prey. The Rose-Hair Tarantula is a particularly docile and slow-moving species, making it a favorite in the exotic pet trade. The last of the seven leg segments, the tarsus, is covered with hairy claw tufts. These velcro-like pads allow the tarantula to cling easily to the smoothest of surfaces.

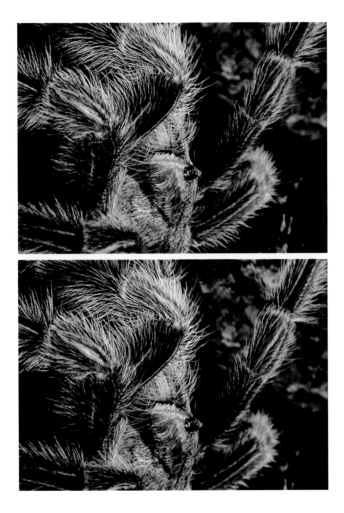

plate 27

gⁱaSshopper

FAMILY ACARIDAE

The jumping characteristics of the grasshopper are renowned. Prior to a jump, the grasshopper may be observed pivoting its body from side to side. In this manner, the image of the landing spot moves across the facets of its compound eyes. By comparing the angles at which light from the landing spot strikes its eyes, the grasshopper can compute the distance it must jump. With the exception of the flightless species ("lubbers"), grasshoppers also use jumping to prime their wings for flight. After a powerful thrust from its hind legs propels the insect into the air, the fanlike hind wings unfurl to provide the lift required for flight.

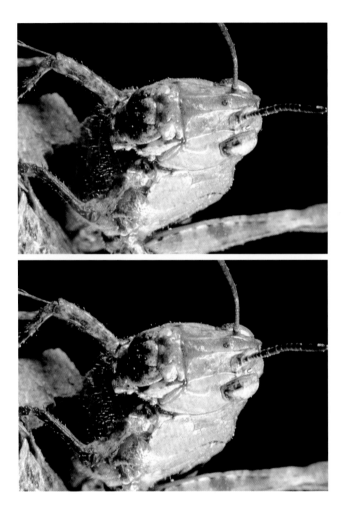

plate 28

giant weevil

MACROCHIRUS PRAETOR

Weevils, also known as snout beetles, are members of the Curculionidae family of beetles. Comprised of more than 40,000 known species distributed throughout the world, Curculionidae is the largest animal family on earth. The weevil's characteristic snout, or rostrum, is an extension of the head and can be three times or more the length of the body. Despite appearances, the snout is not a sucking device. Like all beetles, weevils have a pair of jaws, in this case, located at the tip of the snout. Nearly all species of weevils are plant eaters. Weevil larvae mine, bore, and dig into every plant part, from the roots up to the seeds. Not surprisingly, many weevil species are pests. Adult weevils range in size all the way from ¹⁄₄₀₀th of an inch to 3 inches long. The giant specimen seen here measures about 2½ inches. Its elbowed antennae are also characteristic of weevils.

plate 29

western sand wasp

BEMBIX SP.

Bembix is a member of the Sphecid Wasp family comprised of solitary hunting wasps. Each genus in the family is highly specialized. The common name of the sand wasp derives from its selection of nest burrowing habitat in open sandy areas. The females dig sloping sand tunnels that terminate below the surface in one or more cells. Sand wasps are so fast and agile that they catch flies on the wing. The female paralyzes the fly with her stinger and delivers it to one of the cells she has dug. She then lays one egg on the fly and closes the burrow. When the wasp larva hatches, it begins to feed on the fly. Some species of Bembix continue to bring more flies to the larva as it grows. The full grown larva spins a cocoon in its cell, and later digs its way out as a mature wasp.

plate 30

robber fly

FAMILY ASILIDAE

Robber flies, also known as assassin flies, are fearless hunters of other insects. They will seize out of the air anything that flies by, including much larger wasps, dragonflies, and grasshoppers. The robber fly's sharp, rigid proboscis is a highly evolved killing probe, easily thrust through the toughest exoskeleton. The robber fly injects a neurotoxic saliva through its proboscis that immobilizes the prey and allows the robber fly to drink its juices. Identifying characteristics of the robber fly include a depression between the eyes and the hairy face which is so prominent in this photograph.

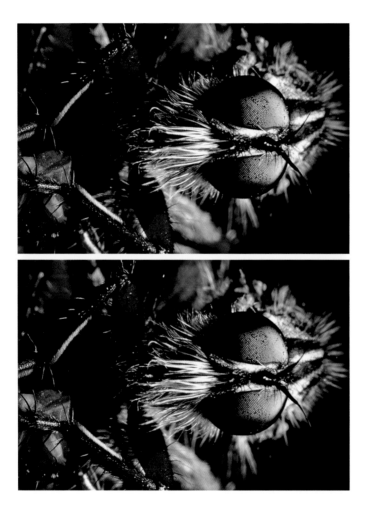

plate 31

c¹cada

CICADIDAE SP.

The 2,500 species in this family are noted for their singing behavior. The raucous sound produced by large tropical species, such as this Malaysian specimen, can be absolutely deafening. The singing is done by the males, whose sound-producing organs, known as tymbals, are found in cavities in the abdomen. Muscles pull on the tymbals, and the resulting sound is amplified by resonating membranes that allow cicadas to modulate their tones. Each species produces recognizably different tones and rhythms. Ironically, while the cacophonous sound of singing cicadas in the wild seems to be everywhere at once, they are shy, hard to locate, and nearly impossible to catch. But time is on the side of the patient observer. Due to the plant feeding cicada's poor diet, development into adulthood can take up to 17 years!

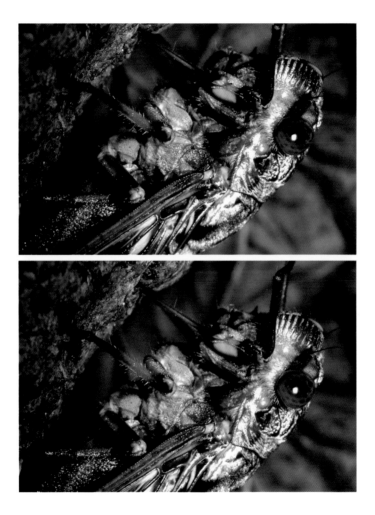

plate 32

shield bug

FAMILY PENTATOMIDAE

The presence of the piercing and sucking mouth part (the rostrum) seen in this picture distinguishes these bugs from all other insects. In the true bugs, such as this specimen, the rostrum is not fixed. The bug can retract it and, more importantly, can control its position. This precision allows the shield bug to exploit a greater range of food sources than all other bugs. Look closely at the tip of the rostrum of this specimen and you will see a drop of fluid, which the shield bug has extracted from a plant. Many species of plant-feeding bugs can seriously damage crops and are considered pests. Some species also transmit plant diseases and at least one, the South American Assassin Bug, carries the organism responsible for Chagas Disease in humans.

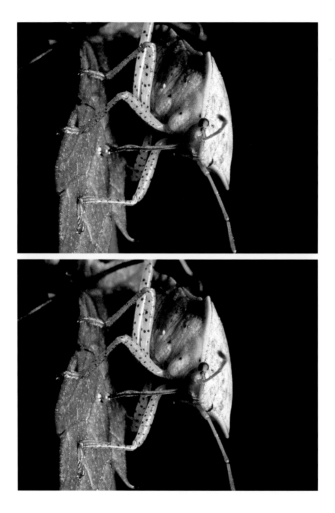

plate 33

honeybee

This species, introduced to North America in the 17th century, is the most widely recognized of the seven honeybee species in the genus Apis. Honeybees are generally considered to be the most advanced of the social insects. A. mellifera lives in perennial colonies comprised of a single queen, up to 2,000 males (drones), and 40,000 to 80,000 sterile female worker bees. All bees are actually descended from carnivorous hunting wasps. Bees probably switched to eating pollen and nectar about 100 million years ago. In the honeybee colony, the worker bees engage in a complex dance that communicates the direction and distance to nectar and pollen sources. The worker bees have a hairy basket (corbiculum) on each hind leg for the gathering of flower pollen. A variable length tongue allows them to extract nectar from the flowers.

plate 34

scorpion vinegaroon

FAMILY THELYPHONISDAE

The Scorpion Vinegaroon is a member of the whip scorpion family. Unlike true scorpions, it has a whip-like tail instead of a stinger at the end of its abdomen. The jaws are located between two pincer-like pedipalps. The Scorpion Vinegaroon hides by day and hunts by night. The first of its four pairs of legs are long antenna-like filaments used as feelers. It is a delight to watch these slow-moving creatures delicately pick their way across the landscape. Whip scorpions are not poisonous, but when provoked many emit a highly concentrated vinegar-like secretion from a gland at the base of the tail as a defensive mechanism. Caution should be exercised because some specimens can spray this acidic fluid into the eyes of a careless handler.

plate 35

paper wasp nest

POLISTES SP.

The complex paper wasp nest, which is never closed, is laboriously constructed of wood fiber chewed with saliva, and assembled papier-mâché fashion. The nest is started by a single female—the queen. Alone, she rears a first generation of all female workers. These worker wasps then take over the queen's other tasks, including expansion of the nest and larval care, so that she can concentrate on egg laying. In the hexagonal cells are the queen's developing wasp larvae. Through aggressive dominance behavior, the queen will prevent most of the female workers from egg laying. Those workers that do lay eggs will produce only male offspring.

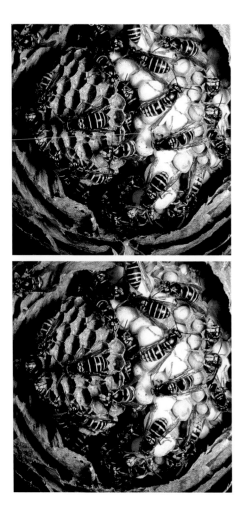

plate 36

crab spider and green bottle fly

FAMILY THOMISIDAE AND PHAENICIA SP.

On this deadly hemlock plant a crab spider has ambushed and poisoned a green bottle fly. In contrast to hunting spiders, the crab spider lies in wait on the flower its coloration so closely resembles, holding out two pairs of bristled front legs. The crab spider does not construct a web. When the prey comes within range, the crab spider grabs it and quickly injects a neurotoxic poison into the back of the victim's neck where the nerve cord passes through. The victim's tissues are dissolved and drawn in through the spider's hollow fangs. The speed of the poisoning and the natural look of the carcass minimize the risk of another predator detecting the spider's presence. Although spiders cannot perceive warning coloration, the crab spider can readily distinguish a desirable hover fly from the deadly bee or wasp that it attempts to mimic.

plate 37

long-horned beetle

BATOCERA SP.

The 25,000 beetle species in the Cerambycidae family are highly diversified and widely distributed. Their sizes range from a mere $^{12}/_{100}$s of inch to an enormous 8 inches long. The pictured specimen from Peninsular Malaysia is approximately 2 inches long. There are many forms of Long-horned beetle that mimic not only the appearance, but in some cases even the behavior of wasps, ants, bugs, and other beetles. In certain instances the mimicing of other species is much more detailed than appears to be required for mere protective value. This phenomenon has caused some entomologists to question the validity of the general theory of mimicry. The active defenses of the Long-horned beetle are limited to its mandibles, which can be formidable in the larger species. The long, curved antennae, sometimes up to five times the insect's body length, lend these beetles a ram-like appearance.

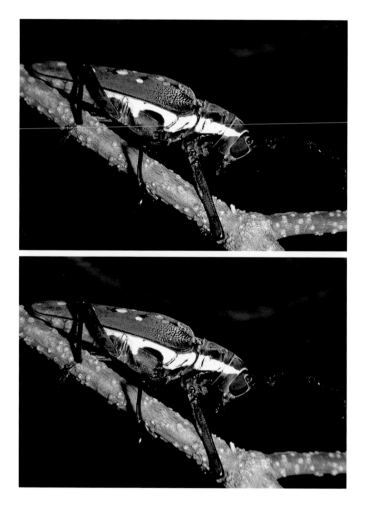

plate 38

moving leaf

PHYLLIUM GIGANTEUM

The fantastic leaf insects, together with their relatives the stick insects, comprise the order Phasmatidae. Derived from Greek, *phasma* means apparition or specter. True to their name, these insects literally appear to be parts of plants. The flightless female Moving Leaf replicates leaves to an astounding level of detail. Notice on the forelegs of this specimen how the veins resemble leaf veins and the ragged brown edges mimic the dead edges of damaged foliage. The various leaf insect species are matched to particular trees, particularly the Cacao tree. They avoid predation by hanging motionless in a trance-like state ("catalepsy"), but they can also emit a corrosive secretion to deter attackers. So convincing is the Moving Leaf's disguise that other insects may mistake them for leaves and bite them. Despite their excellent camouflage, leaf insects reproduce slowly and are uncommon. Males are very rare and new generations of insects can develop from unfertilized eggs.

plate 39

dᵃmselfly

ISCHNURA SP.

Damselflies and dragonflies are the two groups making up the insect order Odonata. Compared to the robust dragonflies, damselflies are relatively frail. They are nevertheless very agile fliers, with the ability to hover, fly backwards, and turn within their own body length. Adult damselflies feed mainly on small flying insects, which they catch in flight. The naiads of the genus Ischnura live in the water and eat aquatic animals. Both the adults and naiads can be found around still, fresh water. Like dragonflies, damselflies can copulate head to tail while flying, an evolutionary device that renders them less vulnerable to predators when mating. The female is ready to lay eggs right after mating.

plate 40

common checker-spot butterfly

OCCIDRYAS CHALCEDONA

Butterflies are capable of seeing red, green, and yellow, and use these colorations to communicate information to other members of their species. The wonderful colors and patterns observed in the wings of butterflies are created by the wing scales. The source of the scale colors can be plants in the caterpillar's diet, manufactured proteins, or light interference produced by the microstructure of the scales. The head of the butterfly is equipped with well-developed compound eyes, a proboscis for drinking nectar, antennae, and sometimes two simple eyes (ocelli). The club-tipped antennae carry receptors that are highly sensitive to chemical odors (pheromones) emitted by females to attract males of the same species. The Common Checker-spot is generally tolerant of human presence and the slow-moving photographer may often approach closely.

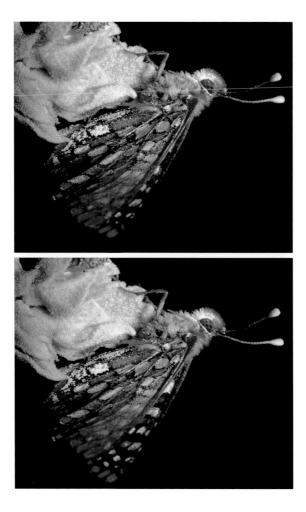

plate 41

muscid fly

FAMILY MUSCIDAE

The large family Muscidae contains many of the most common flies, including the well-known House Fly, *Musca domestica*. The stout, dark hairs on all of the fly's body parts are characteristic of this family. Eggs are laid in all manner of decaying or dead material and develop rapidly. Most muscid flies feed on rotting matter or flower nectar, which they absorb with sponge-like mouth parts. Other species, however, are blood-suckers with piercing mouth parts. These flies are reported to transmit at least 80 parasitic diseases to humans. Non-biting species such as the House Fly are also disease vectors. They spread typhoid fever, cholera, dysentery, and other illnesses by carrying bacteria, viruses, and parasitic worms on their feet and mouths.

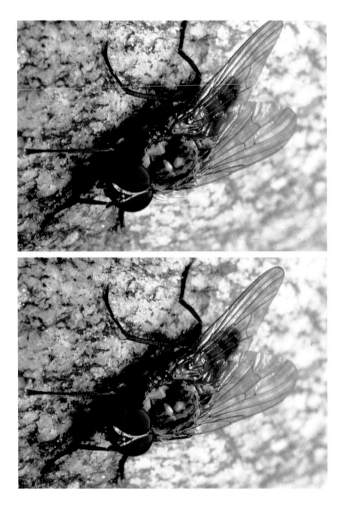

plate 42

molting orb weaver spider

FAMILY ARANEIDAE

Like insects and crustaceans, spiders must molt (ecdysis) their rigid exoskeletons in order to grow into adults. This orb weaver spider has just shed its old exoskeleton, leaving it hanging from a silk thread. It must now expand the new skeleton to its full size while flexing its joints so they will remain supple. Molting is dangerous, because the spider is vulnerable to many predators during the process. Depending on the size of the species, spiders must molt three to ten times, with the larger spiders requiring more molts. The sex of the spider only becomes obvious after the last molt into maturity. Some large tarantulas, which may live up to 25 years, must continue to molt even after reaching mature form.

plate 43

mating leaf beetles

MELASOMA SP.

In this mating pair of leaf beetles, the specialized feet of the male act like suction pads, allowing him to hold on to the slippery back of the female. Beetles are exceptionally well-adapted for survival on the ground. If success can be estimated in numbers, then beetles, representing over 30 percent of all described animal species, are overwhelming winners. Six legs carry beetles over and under all manner of terrain, while hind wings power their flight. The forewings have evolved into elytra, tough protective cases sheltering the delicate hind wings. Beetle flight begins with a leap into the air. At the proper moment, the elytra lift away and the hind wings unfold. If the movements are out of sync, the attempted flight fails, and the process must be repeated.

plate 44

african praying mantis

MANTIS SP.

The common name, praying mantis, is derived from the prayer-like posture in which the praying mantis holds its barbed front legs as it waits for prey. The ability of the praying mantis to hang motionlessly for long periods of time effectively renders it invisible to the eyes of insects, which are sensitive to motion. Stereoscopic vision allows the praying mantis to accurately gauge when potential prey is within its reach. The snap of the raptorial front legs lasts just $30/1000$ths to $50/1000$ths of a second, and can grasp a flying insect out of the air. In this photograph, the praying mantis is devouring a common household cricket, head first.

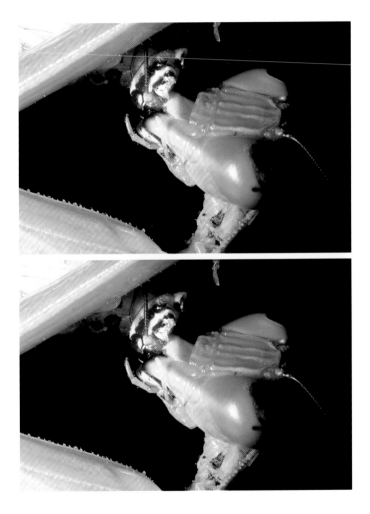

glossary

An **aggregation** is the collection of many individuals into a group.

Antennae are long, slender, flexible sensory organs located on the heads of insects and crustaceans.

An **aquatic** creature is one that lives or grows in or on water.

An **arachnid** is any member of the class of invertebrates that have a segmented body divided into two regions, having four pairs of legs but no antennae. Spiders, scorpions, mites, and ticks are arachnids.

An **arthropod** is any member of the phylum arthropoda that includes insects, crustaceans, and arachnids.

A **booklung** is a sacklike respiratory organ found in some arachnids. It is folded in a way that resembles the leaves of a book.

Bug is the common name for the entire insect order Hemiptera.

The **cephalothorax** is a body section composed of the fused head and thorax in crustacea and chelicerate arthropods.

Chelicerate arthropods comprise a subphylum of arthropods usually having two body regions, such as arachnids.

Chitin is a semitransparent horny substance that is the chief component of crustacean shells and insect exoskeletons.

Chrysalis is the third stage in the development of a moth or butterfly, when it is encased in a case or cocoon.

Class is a category used to classify animals. **Order, family, genus,** and **species** are other categories of biological classification.

Corbiculae are basketlike structures for collecting pollen, and are found on the hind legs of honeybees.

Cuticle is a mixture of chitin and proteins that forms the basis of many arthropod structures, including the exoskeleton, hairs, scales, and sense organs.

An **entomologist** is a scientist who studies insects.

The **exoskeleton** is the external supportive covering of an arthropod.

Genus is a category of biological classification, ranking between the **family** and the **species.**

Halteres are club-tipped structures evolved from the hind wings of flies, which help them to balance and change direction while flying.

Invertebrate is the general name for any of the millions of kinds of animals that do not have a backbone. Insects, crustaceans, and arachnids are invertebrates.

The **labium** is a liplike structure found on the mouth in insects.

Larva is the wingless, often wormlike form of a newly hatched insect with complete metamorphosis.

The **mandible** and the **maxillae** are parts of an insect's mouth.

Molting refers to the shedding of an outer covering as part of an organism's growth process.

Nectar is a sweet liquid secreted by various flowers.

A **neurotoxic** substance is one that is poisonous to the nerves or nervous tissue.

A **nymph** is an insect at a stage of metamorphosis between larva and adult form, sometimes called a **naiad.**

Order is a category for the classification of living things, below the **class** and above the **family.**

Ovaries are the female reproductive glands in which eggs are produced.

To **oviposit** is to lay eggs.

A **parasite** is a living thing that feeds off another organism while living on or inside it, often harming the host animal in the process.

Pedipalps are the appendages in chelicerate anthropods that are adapted for various sensory functions.

Pheromones are chemical substances secreted by an animal to influence the behavior of other members of the same species.

Phylum is one of the primary divisions of the animal kingdom.

A **predator** is an animal that captures and eats other animals; this behavior is described as **predacious.**

The **proboscis** is a slender, tubular feeding structure of some insects and worms.

Pupa is the inactive stage in the metamorphosis of many insects, following the larval stage and coming before the adult form.

Raptor is another name for a predator.

The **rostrum** is a beak for piercing and sucking.

A **species** is a group of plants or animals that breed with one another and share physical characteristics.

Spinnerets are organs in a spider or caterpillar that produce threads of silk.

The **thorax** is the middle section of the body of an arthropod.

The **tracheae** are air ducts.

A **vector** is an organism that carries disease from one animal to another.

index

about the author

Mark Blum has been photographing the world in three dimensions for twenty-nine years. From his beginnings with a Stereo Realist camera, he has gone on to design his own equipment for the specialized demands of 3-D wildlife photography. Mark works both as a stock photographer and on assignment around the globe, emphasizing natural history subjects. He is best known for his pioneering work in underwater stereo photography. Mark's extraordinary marine images have been published on CD and in three books of his collected stereographs, including *Beneath the Sea in 3-D* from Chronicle Books. He makes his home on Monterey Bay in Pacific Grove, California.